SEARCH FOR HONEY

Pooh is ready for a snack!
Help him find the correct path to his honey jar.

Answer: C is the correct path.

MR. SANDERS

POT PAINTING

Pooh's friends want to surprise him with a new honey pot! Add your own creative touch to the one below using colour, shapes, patterns and anything else you can imagine.

DOT-TO-DOT

Starting at one, draw a line to join the dots and finish this picture of Tigger.

RABBIT'S GARDEN

Rabbit and Roo are picking apples in Rabbit's garden.
How many apples are still in the tree?

There are ________ apples in the tree.

Answer: There are 8 apples in the tree.

PIGLET'S ART
Piglet is creating a masterpiece, but what is he painting?
Draw it on his easel. Then, colour the rest of the scene!
© 2026 Disney. Based on the 'Winnie the Pooh' works by A.A. Milne and E.H. Shepard.
10

HONEY PATH
Pooh is out of honey! Help him through the maze below to refill his honey pot.
START
FINISH
Answers on the last page.
© 2026 Disney. Based on the "Winnie the Pooh" works by A.A. Milne and E.H. Shepard.
12

WORD SEARCH

Can you find the names of these Winnie the Pooh characters?
Words can go forwards and backwards, vertically and horizontally.

G B J W M X Q H S A G W V H C
F W K P J P G F T G F E Z Y H
K O V D D H Q X O W J R O U V
Z E R H P T B N C Q A S V A G
Z G B C Z E E D L E V I I F R
K Q M E M O Q L L L S E Y E L
H V W Z B W N C G K U F H X U
F U G G A L O T U I A E Z L M
G R L W E J G D R E P N Z H P
P V A M W W D N X X C D G Z Y
P Q M B M P X Y R D A A Y A X
L O M R B F I E R O Y E E C N
Y E F Q T I G G E R O W D X X
V Q M J R O T J B B M H O O P
V K I A L L S G N F J N P W C

Eeyore
Kanga
Lumpy
Owl
Piglet
Pooh
Rabbit
Roo
Tigger

Answers on the last page.

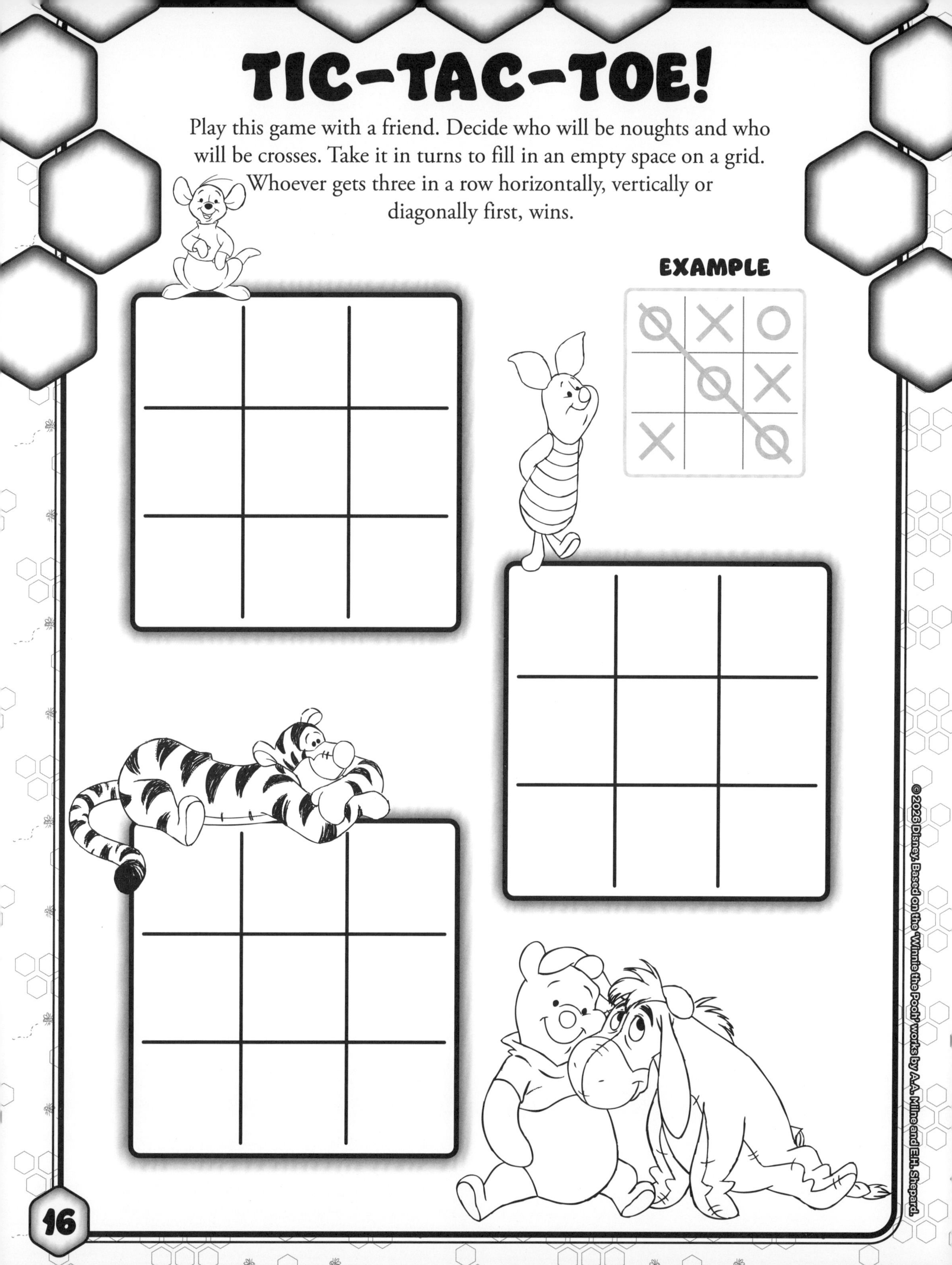

TIC-TAC-TOE!
Play this game with a friend. Decide who will be noughts and who will be crosses. Take it in turns to fill in an empty space on a grid. Whoever gets three in a row horizontally, vertically or diagonally first, wins.
EXAMPLE
© 2026 Disney. Based on the "Winnie the Pooh" works by A.A. Milne and E.H. Shepard.
16

CROSSWORD
Complete the crossword by filling in all the names from the word bank below.
Some letters have been done for you!
H
I
K
E
T
O
ACROSS
OWL
EEYORE
TIGGER
DOWN
HONEY
PIGLET
KANGA
ROO
Answers on the last page.
18
© 2026 Disney. Based on the "Winnie the Pooh" works by A.A. Milne and E.H. Shepard.

ANAGRAMS

How many words can you make by rearranging the letters in:

WINNIE THE POOH

Answers include: Hen; Honey; Hope; How; New; One; Phone; When; Whiney; Who.

HONEY SEARCH

There are multiple jars of honey hidden in the image below.
How many can you find and circle?

There are __________ jars of honey!

Answer: There are 11 jars of honey.

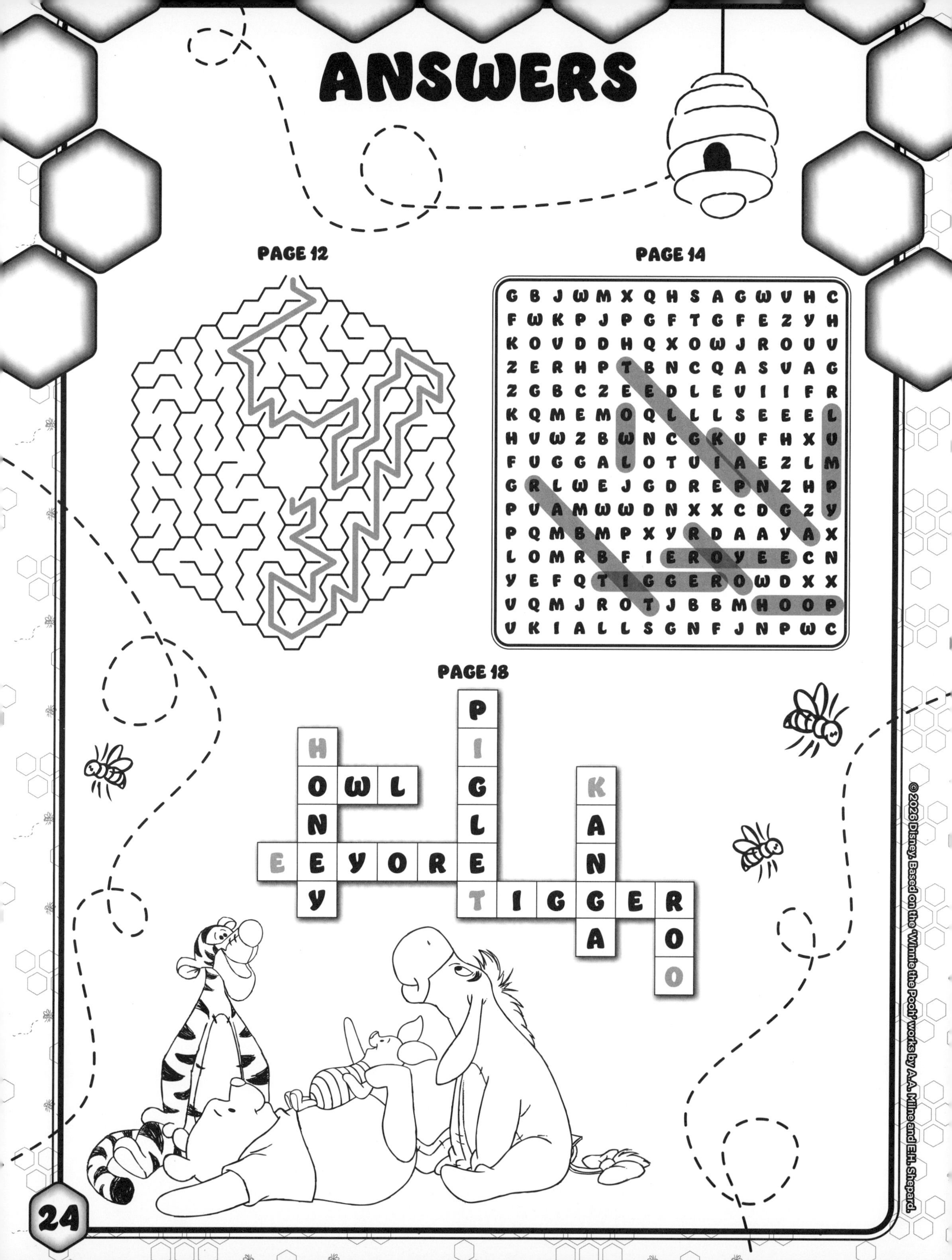
ANSWERS
PAGE 12
PAGE 14
G B J W M X Q H S A G W V H C
F W K P J P G F T G F E Z Y H
K O V D D H Q X O W J R O U V
Z E R H P T B N C Q A S V A G
Z G B C Z E E D L E V I I F R
K Q M E M O Q L L L S E E E L
H V W Z B W N C G K U F H X U
F U G G A L O T U I A E Z L M
G R L W E J G D R E P N Z H P
P V A M W W D N X X C D G Z Y
P Q M B M P X Y R D A A Y A X
L O M R B F I E R O Y E E C N
Y E F Q T I G G E R O W D X X
V Q M J R O T J B B M H O O P
V K I A L L S G N F J N P W C
PAGE 18
HONEY
OWL
PIGLET
KANGA
EEYORE
TIGGER
ROO